D0835367

Published by Ladybird Books Ltd.,
80 Strand, London WC2R 0RL
A Penguin Company
Penguin Books Australia Ltd., Camberwell, Victoria, Australia
Penguin Books (NZ) Ltd., Private Bag 102902, NSMC,
Auckland, New Zealand

2 4 6 8 10 9 7 5 3 1

Printed in Italy

With love on Mother's Day

Ladybird

It's a special
day for mums
everywhere.

A time for
children to
tell them
they care.

You make me
smile and
laugh all
the day.

You teach me
to be kind,
to learn
and to play.

Always be
close, mum,
let's never
be apart.

The best
place to be
is close to
your heart.

Mum,
this is a
special hug,
just to say . . .

. . . I'll always
love you.
Happy
Mother's
Day!